The Truth about
CHUCK NORRIS

The Truth about

CHUCK

NORRIS

**400 Facts
about the
WORLD'S
GREATEST
HUMAN**

Ian Spector

GOTHAM
BOOKS

GOTHAM BOOKS

Published by Penguin Group (USA) Inc.
375 Hudson Street, New York, New York 10014, U.S.A.
Penguin Group (Canada), 90 Eglinton Avenue East, Suite 700, Toronto, Ontario M4P
2Y3, Canada (a division of Pearson Penguin Canada Inc.); Penguin Books Ltd, 80
Strand, London WC2R 0RL, England; Penguin Ireland, 25 St Stephen's Green, Dublin 2,
Ireland (a division of Penguin Books Ltd); Penguin Group (Australia), 250 Camberwell
Road, Camberwell, Victoria 3124, Australia (a division of Pearson Australia Group
Pty Ltd); Penguin Books India Pvt Ltd, 11 Community Centre, Panchsheel Park, New
Delhi–110 017, India; Penguin Group (NZ), 67 Apollo Drive, Rosedale, North Shore
0632, New Zealand (a division of Pearson New Zealand Ltd); Penguin Books (South
Africa) (Pty) Ltd, 24 Sturdee Avenue, Rosebank, Johannesburg 2196, South Africa

Penguin Books Ltd, Registered Offices: 80 Strand, London WC2R 0RL, England

Published by Gotham Books, a member of Penguin Group (USA) Inc.

First printing, November 2007
10 9 8 7 6 5 4 3 2 1

Gotham Books and the skyscraper logo are trademarks of Penguin Group (USA) Inc.

LIBRARY OF CONGRESS CATALOGING-IN-PUBLICATION DATA
Spector, Ian.
The truth about Chuck Norris: 400 facts about the world's greatest human / Ian Spector.
    p.   cm.
ISBN 978-1-592-40344-8 (pbk.)
1. Norris, Chuck, 1940– Humor. 2. Norris, Chuck, 1940– Miscellanea. I. Title.
GV1113.N67S68 2007
796.8092—dc22   2007033896

Printed in the United States of America
Set in Monkton   ·   Designed by Sabrina Bowers

To **ALL OF YOU** who kept the site alive, especially the volunteers (Mike, Brian, Eric, Rob, Alex, and everyone else) who helped to code the Web site and keep it running smoothly.

Preface

As a kid, I always used to skip the prefaces in the comedy books I owned. "Why read what the author has to say? This stuff isn't funny at all," I thought. Hopefully none of you are like me in that respect. Since it's easy enough to copy and paste content from my Web site to fill up the rest of this book, I suppose it might be worthwhile to explain how all of this got started and what I think of it.

In March of 2005, *The Pacifier,* starring Vin Diesel, was released to the masses. Vin was either loved for his badass-ness or mocked for it by most before then, but after that fateful opening weekend most people shifted to the latter camp. One of the Internet forums I visit at SomethingAwful.com had a discussion going where users extrapolated Vin's strange role as Navy–SEAL-turned-babysitter in the form of these very strange "facts."

They were damn entertaining to read (and even more to visualize), and I thought that it would be a fun little project to compile a bunch of them on a Web site that would randomly spit them out. I had purchased a domain name a few weeks earlier and thought it would be as an appropriate place as any to put this thing.

The Web site, www.4Q.cc/vin, started off as a tweaked version of a random quote generator from HotScripts.com. I had posted a link to the generator on SomethingAwful, and within twenty-four hours the site got over twenty thousand hits. The next day I allowed people to submit their own facts and rate facts already on the site. I also put up ads, but never made much off the ad revenue—usually enough to keep things running, but never too much beyond that. The site continued to grow in popularity over the next few months. It was featured on some well-known Web sites like Defamer.com, Empire Online, and ESPN.com, to name a few.

So where does Chuck Norris come into play? Over the summer of 2005, I put up a poll on the site asking visitors who the next fact generator should be about. There were about twelve choices ranging from the entertainment world (Lindsay Lohan, Samuel L. Jackson) to the political (George Bush, Dick Cheney). There was also a space where visitors could write in their own suggestions. After a week of polling, I was surprised to discover that more people had written in "Chuck Norris" than had voted for any of the other twelve. I wasn't very familiar with his work beyond *Dodgeball* and *Walker, Texas Ranger,* so I was hesitant to select him as the next victim.

However, I forged ahead with the Chuck Norris Fact Generator, getting some much-needed technical help from someone who'd created a similar site for Bob Saget, of all people. The site went live in the summer of 2005, and it took a little while to gain momentum. Helped in part by a mention on CollegeHumor.com, however, by early 2006 we were getting nearly twenty million page views per month. Thus began the Chuck Norris global phenomenon.

As the site's editor in chief, so to speak, I spent countless hours wading through the thousands of facts that were submitted. In this task I became quite familiar with the deficits of the American educational system, as I encountered all manner of grammatical nightmares, from confusions of "your" with "you're" to variant spellings of "AIDS" to excessive usage of the exclamation point. Eventually I approved more than ten thousand facts, and a number of copycat sites (all of which stole my content) sprung up all over the Web.

In December of 2005, I had my first chance to meet the man himself. I was asked to appear on CNBC's *The Big Idea with Donny Deutsch* and explain the whole thing to him, because he apparently didn't quite understand it, and I don't really blame him. While I was waiting in the studio, a guy came over to mic me up and I asked, "Does it suck having to watch MSNBC all day long?" He quickly responded, "This is a live mic; you might not want to say that."

Chuck and his wife, Gena, were on the show that day talking about a ton of stuff—his book, his charity, prayer in school. About twenty minutes in, I heard a voice in the earbud that had been implanted by that same guy. It was the director. "Hi, Ian . . . sorry it had to turn out like this, but I'm afraid we're going to have to cut you out for timing. Sorry to make you haul all the way in." I'd like to think that this had nothing to do with my MSNBC joke.

A few weeks later, I was watching *Lost* when my house phone rang. My mom shouted to me, "Ian, pick up the phone!" I refused, because as anyone who watches *Lost* can attest, it's hard to stop watching. Then, she called out, "Ian, *Chuck Norris's wife is on the phone.*" Well, clearly, I put off *Lost* for a few minutes to talk to her. Apparently Chuck's World Combat League was having a fight up at a casino in Connecticut and Chuck wanted me to be there.

The day of reckoning came, and I went up to the Mohegan Sun resort with my dad for the meeting. It ended up being about an hour long or so and included not only myself and Chuck, but also my dad, Chuck's wife Gena, Chuck's lawyer, and Chuck's business manager. Despite those extra folks, we had a pretty interesting conversation ranging from the origins of the site to Chuck's charity (he's really big on it), the Combat League, his book, where the facts originated, my interests, et cetera. I'm still in touch with Chuck and Gena, and to date I've not yet been on the receiving end of a roundhouse kick.

Beyond the Donny Deutsch show, there was a ton of additional media coverage, including a great piece in *The Washington Post*. As a freshman in college, I was pretty wide-eyed about all of it. Thankfully all of the articles written about the site were positive in nature, though there was one that still bothers me to this day: "Heard the One About Chuck Norris?" (February 3, 2006, *St. Petersburg Times*) by "deputy 'Floridian' editor" John Barry. This guy not only called me a "computer geek," but also went on to say the following about me: "Ian looks like what he is, a kid from Rhode Island, studying the supremely esoteric field of 'computational biology.'" Not only did this man get my home state wrong (I'm from New York), he also further perpetuated ignorance by mocking a legitimate and up-coming scientific field. I was really expecting a lot more from the deputy "Floridian" editor.

At the site's peak, I would receive e-mails from fans all over the world. It was a little disturbing to see that there were people from law firms, Fortune 500 companies, major cable networks, and even the London Olympic Committee, who were all wasting time hitting the refresh button on my Web site instead of doing work. One such e-mail was from a visitor from Poland who claimed that Chuck was all the rage in his country. He wasn't kidding. In April 2006, the second most queried phrase on Google from Poland was "Chuck Norris." (Number one was "bird flu.") April is also Chuck's month of birth, and a Polish television station was apparently putting together a special tribute to him and they wanted me to talk about him. They called my cell phone at a ridiculous hour of the night, and a man whose name I could not pronounce and now can't remember asked me three questions and recorded my responses. I never heard from them again, though I wish I could see what they put together.

A radio station in Minnesota had me on the air twice, the second time with Chuck himself. Given the nature of some of the facts, I was pretty scared about his reaction, but he played it cool, which is further testament to his being either a really nice guy or a good actor.

It was in the spring of 2006 when I began getting offers for book versions of the Web site, but I turned them down since I didn't know how much of my time it would take up. It wasn't until late August that I got an e-mail from an agent at the William Morris Agency, one of the top talent agencies for just about anything, asking if I would reconsider doing the book since apparently there were a few publishers who were still very interested. After reading the message, I figured that some people really did want this book, and so I was hooked. My parents, both of whom are overly cautious attorneys, were less enthusiastic about the whole thing, though. After several months of stalling, I wrote all of this up in an all-nighter (it's really surprising what a venti white mocha from Starbucks can do), and here we are.

I've been very lucky with all of this from day one and I doubt I'll ever be this lucky again, so please, tell all your friends to go and buy a copy of this book.

When an episode of *Walker, Texas Ranger* aired in France, the French surrendered to Chuck Norris just to be on the safe side.

Guns don't kill people, Chuck Norris does.

Chuck Norris can eat just one Lay's potato chip.

Chuck Norris killed the pope with a roundhouse kick to the chest after an argument over who had a better beard, Jesus or Norris.

Chuck Norris is strong enough to punch through steel, yet delicate enough to cradle a newborn to sleep.

Chuck Norris got drunk and fucked the Statue of Liberty, then bragged about it to the Lincoln Memorial.

When Chuck Norris bleeds, oak trees sprout up from where the blood fell.

Chuck Norris never hides, he only seeks.

Chuck Norris is so smart, Stephen Hawking stood up to bow down to him.

Ever see the Grand Canyon? Chuck Norris had nothing to do with it, he just went there once on a family vacation.

Rather than being birthed like a normal child, Chuck Norris instead decided to punch his way out of his mother's womb. Hence the term "C-section."

Chuck Norris can fit five billiard balls in his mouth.

Chuck Norris was born of the Greek gods Ares and Hermes in a grand session of butt sex that may never be equaled.

The only person to ever beat Chuck Norris in a game of rock-paper-scissors was a Mexican astronaut that went by the alias "Eduardo the Magnificent."

Occasionally Chuck Norris will call up the Power Rangers just to say hi.

Chuck Norris eats pencils and markers for breakfast, and he shits out masterpieces.

The book of Revelation was actually written by Chuck Norris in a moment of prophecy.

In one episode of *The Fresh Prince of Bel-Air*, Chuck Norris replaced Carlton for a whole scene and nobody noticed.

Chuck Norris once shot a German plane down with his finger by pointing at it and yelling, *"BANG!"*

Chuck Norris can stop time for up to two hours by thinking about pineapples.

Chuck Norris punched a woman in the vagina when she didn't give him exact change.

Chuck Norris, when clean-shaven, radiates the heat of three suns.

Chuck Norris was the first person to tame a dinosaur.

Chuck Norris has no concept of time; if you go to his house you won't find a single clock. When you ask to leave because it's getting late he stares at you blankly until you sit back down.

Chuck Norris once told his moustache to strangle an entire Vietnamese village.

Chuck Norris had no costars on the set of *Walker, Texas Ranger*. He played every role, even the hot chick.

Every piece of furniture in Chuck Norris's house is a Total Gym.

If you can see Chuck Norris, he can see you. If you can't see Chuck Norris, you may be only seconds away from death.

Chuck Norris's body hair is ten times stronger than spider silk and fifty times stickier.

If you've ever met a woman with crooked teeth, you've met a woman who has given Chuck Norris a blowjob.

Chuck Norris was the Jewish Humanitarian of the Year. (Seriously.)

Chuck Norris is just like you and me: He puts his pants on one leg at a time. Except when he puts his pants on, he fights North Koreans.

Who are Chuck Norris's parents? Might, Justice, and Cunning. Yes, all three.

Chuck Norris once boned the Mona Lisa, which is why she smiles.

Contrary to popular belief, Chuck Norris was dropped at Hiroshima and Nagasaki.

Chuck Norris was once accused of heresy by the pope, but as it turns out, Chuck Norris is, in fact, the true son of God.

Chuck Norris's heart beats once every week.

Chuck Norris's dog is trained to pick up his own poop because Chuck Norris will not take shit from anyone.

Chuck Norris is the world's best actor because his moustache is the world's best acting coach.

In Indochina, Chuck Norris's left testicle is worshiped as the god of love, whereas his right testicle is viewed as a fire-breathing demon from hell.

If Chuck Norris had a dollar and you had a dollar, Chuck would kick your ass and take your dollar.

The role of Alf, from the hit eighties TV show of the same name, was actually played by Chuck Norris's penis.

To prove it isn't that big of a deal to beat cancer, Chuck Norris smoked fifteen cartons of cigarettes a day for two years and acquired seven different kinds of cancer only to rid them from his body by flexing for thirty minutes. Beat that, Lance Armstrong.

Chuck Norris would hit that.

Chuck Norris will never fully be male nor female. Doctors once asked him which he preferred. He gave them an ad for a Total Gym.

If Chuck Norris had a dime for every man that didn't die from his roundhouse kick, he would have no dimes.

Chuck Norris just pissed your pants.

Chuck Norris keeps a horde of trained bees under his beard to let loose at a moment's notice.

Chuck Norris invented babies because he got tired of eating the same old thing.

The chief export of Chuck Norris is pain.

Chuck Norris began the Church of England in 1799, back when his nickname was "England."

Chuck Norris is considered a prime number in certain schools in Ontario.

Chuck Norris lives by only one rule: No Asian Chicks.

When Chuck Norris was denied a McGriddle at McDonald's because it was 10:35, he roundhouse kicked the store so hard it became a Wendy's.

Chuck Norris's poop is used as currency in Argentina.

When Chuck Norris punches you in the uterus, you become pregnant. Don't try an abortion, either; it only makes the fetus stronger.

Chuck Norris wears a live rattlesnake as a condom.

Chuck Norris can make a woman climax by simply pointing at her and saying, "Booya."

Chuck Norris is not a man; he is the culmination of hundreds of years of black oppression.

Chuck Norris's penis is so large that it actually warps the fabric of space-time. Indeed, some researchers now theorize that the passage of time is merely a by-product of Norris's colossal erections. This is known as the "Chuck Norris's Big Cock Theory of Space-Time" and is steadily gaining acceptance among physicists.

The National Funeral Directors Association voted to make Chuck Norris their honorary president after he personally increased their business by 300 percent.

Chuck Norris is the only person ever capable of telling if an aircraft landed in soil by tasting it.

Chuck Norris invented the measurement the "yard," as it was much easier to say than, "Hi, my name is Chuck Norris and my dick is three feet long."

Chuck Norris can make the Kessel Run in less than ten parsecs.

Chuck Norris's dick is so big, it has its own dick. And Chuck Norris's dick's dick is bigger than your dick.

In China there is an ancient legend that one day a child will be born from a dragon and vanquish evil from the land. That man is not Chuck Norris, but Chuck Norris did kill that man.

Chuck Norris once inhaled a seagull.

The Great Wall of China was modeled after Chuck Norris's pectoral muscles. This explains the large number of dead Asians buried within the wall.

Chuck Norris's advice?
GROW A BEARD.

Chuck Norris once ejaculated solid gold into a river in India, bringing profit to the local villagers and causing him to be worshiped as a god.

They use Chuck Norris's foreskin as a tarp when it rains at Yankee Stadium.

Chuck Norris cultivates a small population of third-world orphans with red hair so he can harvest them at a moment's notice for his beard.

If someone asks Chuck Norris what his favorite song is, he roundhouse kicks them in the face until they beg for mercy. He then tells them that's music to his ears.

Chuck Norris's tears cure cancer. Too bad he has never cried. ⟶

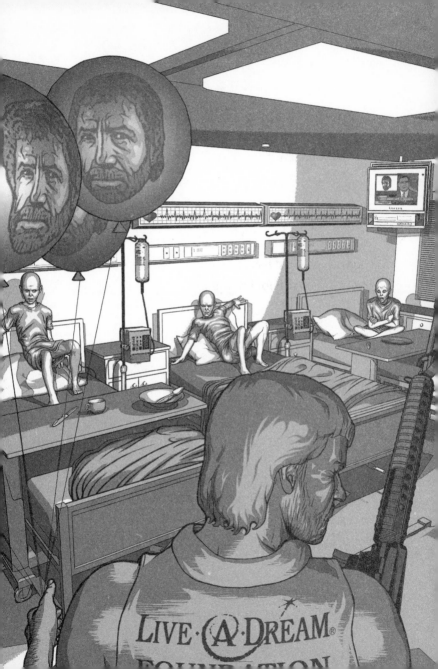

Chuck Norris was voted "Most likely to save a POW using a mule kick" by his senior class.

Chuck Norris doesn't believe in Germany.

As well as being an actor, martial artist, and poet, Chuck Norris is also a world-renowned physicist. It was in this capacity that he once had a disagreement about steady-state theory with Stephen Hawking. Hence the wheelchair.

At Chuck Norris's bachelor party, he ate the entire cake before his friends could tell him there was a stripper in it.

When Chuck Norris's wife burned the turkey one Thanksgiving, Chuck said, "Don't worry about it, honey," and went into his backyard. He came back five minutes later with a live turkey, ate it whole, and, when he threw it up a few seconds later, it was fully cooked and came with cranberry sauce. When his wife asked him how he had done it, he gave her a roundhouse kick to the face and said, "Never question Chuck Norris."

Chuck Norris bemoans the fact that the typical American is unaware that *Walker, Texas Ranger* is an unscripted reality show.

Chuck Norris exists only because he kicked a man so hard that he flew back in time and fell in love with his mother.

Chuck Norris is the only
100 percent effective form of
contraception.

For Chuck Norris, pimping is easy.

Chuck Norris has a Wrangler belt in karate.

While not officially a diplomat, Chuck Norris has his own seat at the United Nations. He walked into the building by accident in 1992 and sat down in a seat reserved for the representative from Denmark, who chose to sit cross-legged on the floor rather than risk asking him to leave.

Chuck Norris makes onions cry.

Chuck Norris can impregnate women with only a glance. He can also do this to men.

Instead of warming up before a workout, Chuck Norris hammers himself to a crucifix and then pulls the stakes out with his teeth.

Chuck Norris eats coal and shits diamonds.

Instead of having a cigarette after sex, Chuck Norris heads outside and brands his cattle.

Chuck Norris defeated Hulk Hogan at the Battle of Little Big Horn.

Chuck Norris is currently suing NBC, claiming "Law" and "Order" are trademarked names for his left and right legs.

Chuck Norris once donated ten liters of his own blood. After that he won the Tour de France on a pogo stick.

Chuck Norris once ate three seventy-two-ounce steaks in one hour. He spent the first forty-five minutes of that hour having sex with his waitress.

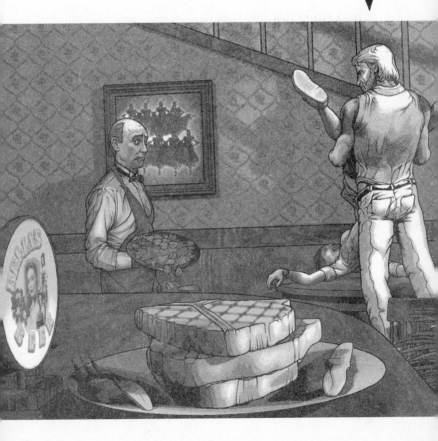

Chuck Norris was the fourth wise man. He brought baby Jesus the gift of "beard." Jesus wore it proudly to his dying day. The other wise men, jealous of Chuck, used their combined influence to have him omitted from the Bible. Shortly thereafter, all three died roundhouse kick–related deaths.

Chuck Norris caddied for the Dalai Lama once. Instead of giving him money, the Lama offered Chuck the ability to receive total consciousness on his deathbed. Clearly upset by this offer, Chuck roundhouse kicked him into a 10,000-foot crevasse.

Chuck Norris once roundhouse kicked someone so fast that they actually grew younger.

Chuck Norris plans to assassinate four other civil rights leaders just to get an entire week off in February.

Chuck Norris once made love to a grizzly bear for four hours.

Chuck Norris trims his beard with a dull bayonet.

Chuck Norris coined the phrase, "Don't come near me, motherfucker, or I'll roundhouse kick the shit out of you." The phrase has since been changed to, "Don't mess with Texas."

It never rains on Chuck Norris.

Chuck Norris can eat a Rubik's Cube and poop it out solved.

Chuck Norris's penis has a toenail.

Chuck Norris's girlfriend once asked him how much wood a woodchuck could chuck if a woodchuck could chuck wood. Chuck then shouted, *"How dare you rhyme in the presence of Chuck Norris!"* and ripped out her throat. Holding his girlfriend's bloody throat in his hand, he bellowed, *"Don't fuck with Chuck!"* Two years and five months later he realized the irony of this statement and laughed so hard that anyone within a hundred-mile radius of the blast went deaf.

Chuck Norris came up with the idea for the Total Gym after trying to bench press his own penis. He found that he needed to start with a lighter weight and work his way up.

Chuck Norris can make your nose bleed with his mind.

Chuck Norris fucked your wife while you were out of town on a business trip. Tough shit.

Chuck Norris sold his soul to the devil for his rugged good looks and unparalleled martial-arts ability. Shortly after the transaction was finalized, Chuck roundhouse kicked the devil in the face and took his soul back. The devil, who appreciates irony, couldn't stay mad and admitted he should have seen it coming. They now play poker every second Wednesday of the month.

Chuck Norris isn't God, but he beats him in golf.

It is commonly known that Eve was created from the rib of Adam, but few know that Chuck Norris was actually created using Adam's genitals.

Chuck Norris's belly button is an "innie." Inside Chuck's belly button is an alternate universe where thousands of tiny Chuck Norrises are training to get their buddies out of a Vietcong POW camp.

Some people eat pepperoni on their pizza. Some people have mushrooms. Chuck Norris usually has Venezuela.

It takes fourteen puppeteers to make Chuck Norris smile, but only two to make him destroy an orphanage.

While Chuck Norris was on holiday in Spain, he ate some bad paella, causing him to take the largest shit known to man. That shit is now France.

When Chuck Norris farts, it smells like freshly baked cinnamon rolls.

Chuck Norris is so fast, he can run around the world and punch himself in the back of the head.

Every cell in Chuck Norris's body has its own beard.

Chuck Norris is where babies come from.

Chuck Norris is the reason why bad things happen to good people.

When he is alone at night, Chuck Norris likes to wear slippers with bunnies on them. Real live bunnies.

Rainbows are what happens when Chuck Norris roundhouse kicks Richard Simmons. ——————————▶

If you drop a phonograph needle on Chuck Norris's nipple, it plays the Beach Boys' *Pet Sounds*.

Chuck Norris can lift a mountain over his head with one arm and make a perfect pitcher of Kool-Aid with the other.

Chuck Norris can charge a cell phone just by rubbing it against his beard.

A recent poll discovered 93 percent of women think about Chuck Norris during sex. A related poll discovered Chuck Norris thinks about Chuck Norris 100 percent of the time during sex.

Chuck Norris refers to himself in the fourth person.

Chuck Norris once leaned against a tower in Pisa, Italy.

There are three ways to do things: the right way, the wrong way, and the Chuck Norris way. The Chuck Norris way is the same as the wrong way, but with more roundhouse kicks.

Chuck Norris can travel through time by running at eighty-eight miles per hour.

Chuck Norris's family crest is a picture of a barracuda eating Neil Armstrong.

Chuck Norris once roundhouse kicked someone so hard that his foot broke the speed of light, went back in time, and killed Amelia Earhart while she was flying over the Pacific Ocean.

Whenever Chuck Norris makes a joke, the sound of an audience laughing comes from out of nowhere. Chuck will then turn to you, smile, and give you two thumbs-up. After that, everything freezes; even *you* are unable to move. The laughter then turns into music as credits begin to scroll down from thin air. Finally, your sight fades to black and there is nothing. When you regain your vision and mobility, Chuck Norris is nowhere to be found.

The only reason it is not called *The CBS Evening News with Chuck Norris* is that Dan Rather once pulled a thorn out of Chuck's paw.

Chuck Norris has three birthdays a year.

Chuck Norris's blood type is D.O.A.

When the Incredible Hulk gets angry he turns into Chuck Norris.

Chuck Norris doesn't have normal white blood cells like you and me. His have a small black ring around them. This signifies that they are black belts and they roundhouse kick the shit out of viruses. That's why Chuck Norris never gets ill.

By presidential decree, every time Chuck Norris trims his beard, the whiskers are gathered and buried at Arlington Cemetery with full honors.

Chuck Norris owns the greatest poker face of all time. It helped him win the 1983 World Series of Poker despite him holding just a joker, a Get Out of Jail Free Monopoly card, a 2 of clubs, a 7 of spades, and a green number 4 card from the game Uno.

Chuck Norris performs back-alley abortions with his beard.

The heavens parted, the seas quieted, the earth stood still. From her womb, the goddess brought forth Chuck Norris, sired by the sun, as a gift to mankind. He reclined upon the fertile soil under the crescent moon and immediately sprouted a beard. She spoke softly to the young child and said, "Go forth and roundhouse kick people in the face." So it was spoken, and so he does. Every now and then he also sells exercise equipment and wears awesome clothes.

When Chuck Norris has a good idea, he raises a forklift carrying a pallet of light bulbs over his head.

Chuck Norris choked an estimated 400,000 Vietcong to death in 1985.

The only way Chuck Norris can climax is if there's a Vietnamese family begging for their lives nearby.

In Chuck Norris's homeland, a roundhouse kick to the face is equivalent to a handshake.

Chuck Norris's left testicle was declared the Milky Way's tenth planet in 1978. His right testicle remains the Duke of the Thirteenth Republic of South Greenwich.

Superman owns a pair of Chuck Norris pajamas. ⟶

Chuck Norris swears he didn't sleep with your wife. Yes, it is strange that your children show an affinity for Texas justice and beard cultivation. No, Chuck Norris does not know why your wife can only climax when you wear a karate uniform. Chuck Norris thinks you are asking the kind of questions a person asks when they want to be roundhouse kicked in the face.

Chuck Norris drives a pickup truck upholstered in denim.

Chuck Norris took my virginity, and he will sure as hell take yours. If you're thinking to yourself, *"That's impossible, I already lost my virginity,"* then you are dead wrong.

Chuck Norris can grate fresh Parmesan cheese with his rust-red beard.

Chuck Norris fought Gandhi in the very first Ultimate Fighting Championship and won in less than fifteen seconds by crushing Gandhi's rib cage with a single punch. Later, officials questioned the validity of the match, as it took place in Gandhi's home, while he was asleep.

Contrary to popular belief, Chuck Norris, not the blue-ringed octopus of eastern Australia, is the most venomous creature on earth. Within three minutes of being bitten, a human being experiences the following symptoms: fever, blurred vision, beard rash, tightness of the jeans, and the feeling of being repeatedly kicked through a car windshield.

Chuck Norris used to be a regular guest on *Sesame Street*, until Snuffleupagus accidentally ate Chuck's sandwich. Many Muppets died that day.

In an alternate universe, the clean-shaven Chuck Norris of the 1970s is engaged in an epic battle with the bearded Chuck Norris of the eighties and nineties. The result of this conflict is the aurora borealis.

Chuck Norris carved Mount Rushmore by himself with his teeth. It took him thirty seconds.

When you look back and see only one set of footprints,
that's when Chuck Norris was carrying you.

The only reason World War II occurred was because Chuck Norris was taking a nap.

If the coach had put Chuck Norris in in the fourth quarter,
they would have won State. No doubt about it.

If you unscramble the letters in "Chuck Norris" you get "Huck corn, sir." That is why every fall Chuck travels to Nebraska and burns the entire state down.

Chuck Norris roundhouse kicked Jimmy Hoffa into the future. In the year 2052, Hoffa will reappear and crash through the windshield of a flying car.

Chuck Norris eats babies and shits Delta Force team members.

Chuck Norris took three of every animal on his ark. Then he called Noah a pussy and roundhouse kicked a Minotaur.

Chuck Norris was one of the original members of Wu-Tang Clan, but quit because they weren't street enough.

Chuck Norris had sex with your mom, and your dad gave him a high-five.

Chuck Norris gargles with antifreeze.

Chuck Norris can slam a revolving door.

Chuck Norris's beard has a representative in Congress.

Chuck Norris once wrestled a bear, an alligator, and a mountain lion all at once. He won by tying them together with an anaconda. ⟶

Chuck Norris ends every relationship with, "It's not me, it's you."

The movie *Rambo: First Blood* was inspired by Chuck Norris's experiences as a Boy Scout.

Chuck Norris is so fertile that when he bangs a chick in America, a chick in China gets pregnant.

Despite his doctor's and family's strong objections, Chuck Norris began drinking gasoline each morning. Much to everyone's surprise, he gets ninety-four miles per gallon.

Chuck Norris's pubic hair is twice as thick as his beard . . . but not nearly as deadly.

Chuck Norris once ripped a man in half just to see what he had for lunch.

A man once asked Chuck Norris if his real name is "Charles." Chuck Norris did not respond, he simply stared at him until the man exploded.

The Vietnam war ended over thirty years ago. Nobody told Chuck Norris.

Alien vs. Predator is an autobiographical depiction of Chuck Norris's first sexual experience.

Chuck Norris had seven children. Four of them went on to become doctors. The other three were delicious.

A masked man once stabbed Chuck Norris in an alley behind a children's hospital. **THE KNIFE BLED TO DEATH.**

Chuck Norris once roundhouse kicked Bruce Lee, breaking him in half. The result was Jet Li and Jackie Chan.

Chuck Norris owns and operates his own restaurant in Lubbock, Texas. Knuckle sandwiches are the only thing on the menu.

Similar to a Russian nesting doll, if you were to break Chuck Norris open you would find another Chuck Norris inside, only smaller and angrier.

Chuck Norris's genes aren't a double helix. They're barbed wire.

Chuck Norris takes a baseball bat into the bathroom with him in case he craps out a wildcat and has to beat it to death.

Chuck Norris can put a quarter in his ass and then shit out a dime and two nickels. There is a five-cent charge.

When Chuck Norris sends in his taxes, he mails blank forms and includes only a picture of himself, crouched and ready to attack. Chuck Norris has not had to pay taxes ever.

If a tree falls in the middle of a forest and no one is anywhere around, rest assured that Chuck Norris heard it.

If you ask Chuck Norris what time it is, he always says, "Two seconds till." After you ask, "Two seconds till what?" he roundhouse kicks you in the face.

Chuck Norris can turn back time simply by staring at the clock and flexing.

The symbol for Chuck Norris
in sign language is a
middle finger on fire.

If you stare at the American flag long enough, a 3D image
of Chuck Norris pops up.

Chuck Norris once killed a man by simply showing him
how to love.

Chuck Norris has good reasons to believe that Mary was, in fact, not a virgin.

Chuck Norris once tobogganed down Mount Everest and sprinted back to the top when he realized he had lost his mittens.

If Chuck Norris looks at you and even *thinks* about Jesus, you are immediately converted to Christianity.

Chuck Norris was the original Danny Tanner on the hit family sitcom *Full House*. He was replaced by Bob Saget after an unfortunate incident with one of the Olsen triplets. ⟶

Chuck Norris won the Triple Crown last year for the first time since 1978. He needed no horse.

Jesus owns and wears a bracelet that reads, "WWCND?"

The quickest way to a man's heart is with Chuck Norris's fist.

Every dinosaur skull ever found has the imprint of a size fifteen cowboy boot on its jaw. Scientists are baffled, but we know damn well why.

Chuck Norris lost his virginity before his dad did.

Chuck Norris is not hung like a horse . . . horses are hung like Chuck Norris.

Never try to return a Chuck Norris Total Gym. Within sixty seconds of the thought entering your mind, Chuck Norris will rappel through your living-room window, scissor-kick you in the throat, and immediately power-fuck Christie Brinkley on your Total Gym.

Chuck Norris went as Chuck Norris for Halloween. He got twice as much candy as anybody else.

After completing the act of love with Chuck Norris, many women find justice running down their inner thighs.

Chuck Norris's penis is so massive that it has its own elbow.

Chuck Norris's beard conquered Poland three times.

Filming on location for *Walker, Texas Ranger,* Chuck Norris brought a stillborn baby lamb back to life by giving it a prolonged beard rub. Shortly after the farm animal sprang back to life and a crowd had gathered, Chuck Norris roundhouse kicked the animal, breaking its neck, to remind the crew once more that the good Chuck giveth, and the good Chuck, he taketh away.

Someone once tried to tell Chuck Norris that roundhouse kicks aren't the best way to kick someone. This has been recorded by historians as the worst mistake anyone has ever made.

Freddy Krueger has nightmares about Chuck Norris.

Chuck Norris's beard hit .370 in the minors before hurting its knee.

The movie *King Kong* is loosely based on an incident in which Chuck Norris killed a 900-foot gorilla and had sex with the Coors Light twins on the top of the Empire State Building.

The movie *Anaconda* was filmed in Chuck Norris's pants.

Chuck Norris kicked a fifty-yard field goal while having sex.

One time in an airport, a guy accidentally called Chuck Norris "Chick Norris." He explained it was an honest mistake and apologized profusely. Chuck accepted his apology and politely signed an autograph. Nine months later, the guy's wife gave birth to a bearded baby. The guy knew exactly what had happened, and blames nobody but himself.

Chuck Norris does not have normal male nipples. He has a Dodge Ram hood ornament on each pec, and both rams blow smoke out of their noses each and every time he pumps Christie Brinkley.

On the first day, God created the heavens and the earth, looked down, and then said, "Holy shit, is that Chuck Norris?"

Chuck Norris wipes with forty-grit sandpaper.

Chuck Norris's last option is violence. It is also his only option.

Chuck Norris likes his girls like he likes his whiskey— twelve years old and mixed up with coke.

There is no chin behind Chuck Norris's beard. There is only another fist.

Chuck Norris won a staring contest with Medusa. ⟶

A blind man once stepped on Chuck Norris's shoe. Chuck said, "Don't you know who I am? I'm Chuck Norris!" The mere mention of his name cured this man's blindness. Sadly the first, last, and only thing this man ever saw was a fatal roundhouse kick delivered by Chuck Norris.

Chuck Norris is one-eighth Cherokee. This has nothing to do with ancestry; the man ate a fucking Indian.

Chuck Norris doesn't speak. He thinks words towards his foot and then roundhouse kicks them at your brain.

When you open a can of whoop-ass, Chuck Norris jumps out.

The grass is always greener on the other side, unless Chuck Norris has been there. In that case the grass is most likely soaked in blood and tears.

Chuck Norris once got 100 percent on a calculus exam by writing *violence* for every question. Chuck Norris solves all problems with violence.

It's a little known fact that only three things will survive the apocalypse: cockroaches, Chuck Norris, and Chuck Norris's beard.

Chuck Norris once ate an entire factory of sleeping pills. They made him blink.

Chuck Norris once roundhouse kicked cancer so hard he gave it AIDS.

A kid once stole Chuck Norris's hat and ran into an apple orchard. Chuck Norris flew into such a rage that he accidentally invented applesauce.

Chuck Norris can create a rock so heavy that even he can't lift it. And then he lifts it anyway, just to show you who the fuck Chuck Norris is.

If you know someone who doesn't like Chuck Norris, you won't know them for long.

The Virgin Mary saw Chuck Norris in her grilled cheese sandwich.

Chuck Norris blew up the *Challenger* space shuttle. When asked why he said, "I've never left a challenger alive."

For fun, Chuck Norris likes to visit veterinary hospitals. When asked if he has a sick pet, Chuck Norris flexes his biceps and says, "These pythons are pretty sick." He then kisses his arms until all the ladies explode with orgasmic fury.

Chuck Norris does not hunt because the word *hunting* implies the possibility of failure. Chuck Norris goes killing.

When the boogeyman goes to sleep every night he checks his closet for Chuck Norris.

Whenever Chuck Norris's wife asks him nicely to do the dishes, he throws them in the garbage and tells her she looks fat.

A handicap parking sign does not signify that the spot is for handicapped people. It is actually in fact a warning that the spot belongs to Chuck Norris and that you will be handicapped if you park there.

Chuck Norris once played Jenga. The result was the Empire State Building.

When God and Satan play a game of football, Chuck Norris is the field they play upon.

Chuck Norris waited patiently in Al Capone's vault for sixty-three years just so he could give Geraldo Rivera the surprise beating of his lifetime.

How much wood would a woodchuck chuck if a woodchuck could Chuck Norris? All of it.

If the axiom, "You are what you eat" is true, then Chuck Norris is a combination of monster truck tires, Godzilla, and magma from the earth's most active volcanoes.

Chuck Norris clogs the toilet even when he pisses.

Chuck Norris's money shot can actually be counted in $10s and $20s.

Only Wonder Woman has a uterus capable of bearing Chuck Norris's children.

Chuck Norris only allows Jackie Chan to live because he likes Chris Tucker movies.

Chuck Norris eats tiger hearts every morning for strength, power, and wisdom. He eats men's hearts for sport.

Chuck Norris frequently donates blood to the Red Cross. Just never his own.

In order to survive a nuclear attack, you must remember to stop, drop, and be Chuck Norris.

All Chuck Norris wants for Christmas is your two front teeth.

There are two kinds of people in this world: people who are Chuck Norris and people who are going to die.

Chuck Norris remembers the Alamo, and he isn't happy about it.

Chuck Norris solved the Bermuda triangle by using the Pythagorean theorem.

The Bible says Samson killed 15,000 Philistines with the jawbone of an ass. When God asked Chuck Norris what he thought about that, he said, "That's one way to do it." God laughed at Chuck's wisdom, and said, "I knew you were going to say that."

Chuck Norris was supposed to be the next face on Mount Rushmore. Unfortunately granite is not a hard enough material to replicate Chuck Norris's beard.

When Chuck Norris's shit hits the fan, the fan breaks.

As a teen Chuck Norris impregnated every nun in a convent tucked away in the hills of Tuscany. Nine months later the nuns gave birth to the 1972 Miami Dolphins, the only undefeated and untied team in professional football history.

Chuck Norris is so fast he can turn off his bedroom light and be under the covers before the room gets dark.

Chuck Norris doesn't give Christmas presents. If you live to see Christmas, that is your Christmas present from Chuck.

Chuck Norris combs his hair with the teeth of a mighty lion.

When Chuck Norris works out, he sweats fortitude.

Chuck Norris donates all proceeds from the Total Gym to his Children without Beards organization.

Chuck Norris once ordered a Big Mac at Burger King, and got one.

Pee-wee Herman once got arrested for masturbating in public. That same day, Chuck Norris got an award for masturbating in public.

Chuck Norris flosses with barbed wire.

The only thing Chuck Norris ever lost was his virginity.

The day Chuck Norris sleeps with your wife is the happiest day of your life.

Terrorists recently attempted to hijack Chuck Norris's private plane. This resulted in the world record for farthest distance a cowboy boot has been stuck up someone's ass. ⟶

When Chuck Norris enters a night club, he instantly becomes the life of the party. An instant is roughly how long it takes Chuck Norris to kill a room full of people.

Chuck Norris coincidentally lives in a round house.

The only line Chuck Norris stands in is the line of fire.

A good way to tell if you are about to be attacked by Chuck Norris is to notice the music becoming more intense. You might also see ninjas scoping you out from behind trees and on roofs. Death is certain at this point.

Originally Chuck Norris was going to be hired to play the role of Jack Bauer on the show 24. The producers changed their minds when they realized the show would last only seventeen minutes.

Chuck Norris can speak Braille.

Chuck Norris does not know where you live, but he knows where you will die.

There are two types of women: Those who want to sleep with Chuck Norris, and those who want to sleep with Chuck Norris again.

Chuck Norris once had a heart attack; his heart lost.

The saddest moment for a child is not when she learns Santa Claus isn't real, it's when she learns Chuck Norris is. ⟶

Chuck Norris once visited the Virgin Islands. Shortly thereafter, they were renamed The Islands.

Chuck Norris once got in a fight with Lance Armstrong over who had more testicles. Chuck Norris won by three.

Chuck Norris does not leave messages. Chuck Norris leaves warnings.

We all know the magic word is *please*. As in the sentence, "Please don't kill me." Too bad Chuck Norris doesn't believe in magic.

Water boils faster when Chuck Norris watches it.

When Chuck Norris answers the phone, he just says, "Go." This is not permission for you to begin speaking, it is your cue to start running for your life.

Switzerland isn't really neutral. They just haven't figured out what side Chuck Norris is on yet.

It's no coincidence that the tattoo on Mike Tyson's face and the sole of Chuck Norris's boots share the same pattern.

Chuck Norris was once on celebrity *Wheel of Fortune* and was the first to spin. The next twenty-nine minutes of the show consisted of everyone standing around awkwardly, waiting for the wheel to stop.

Chuck Norris shaves with a John Deere tractor.

You may have given your girlfriend a diamond necklace for Christmas, but Chuck Norris gave her a pearl one last night.

Chuck Norris drives Optimus Prime to work.

Chuck Norris once entered a crossword-puzzle contest. He won, and the word *slent* was added to all dictionaries as an acceptable synonym for smell.

As a child, Chuck Norris enjoyed long walks on the beach, particularly Iwo Jima and Normandy.

Chuck Norris once defeated a laser beam in the hundred-meter dash.

Chuck Norris has to maintain a concealed weapon license in all fifty states in order to legally wear pants.

Everything Chuck Norris touches does not turn to gold; instead, it grows a beard.

If Chuck Norris could be any type of tree, he would be titanium.

People say the truth hurts, but it hurts a hell of a lot more when it comes from Chuck Norris.

When Chuck Norris gives you the finger, he's telling you how many seconds you have left to live.

Chuck Norris invented the Internet so people could talk about how great Chuck Norris is.

Chuck Norris is so American, he can eat tyranny and shit apple pie.

Chuck Norris went on *Nickelodeon GUTS* and won all the events without any bungee cords. Then he had sex with Mo on top of the Agro Crag.

Chuck Norris has Braille on his boots so that even blind people will know what's coming.

When Chuck Norris breaks wind, it stays broken.

To show its patriotism, the American flag recently got a tattoo of Chuck Norris.

The fences at the zoo are to keep the animals safe from Chuck Norris.

For some people, one testicle is larger than the other one. For Chuck Norris, each testicle is larger than the other one.

Chuck Norris secretly sleeps with every woman in the world once a month. They bleed for five days as a result.

Chuck Norris puts the **FIST** in **PACIFIST**.

When Chuck Norris goes to the movies, his friends call him "Fire!" because it is safer than saying "Chuck Norris" in a crowd.

All ninety-nine of Jay-Z's problems are Chuck Norris.

When Chuck Norris wants a salad, he eats a vegetarian.

Chuck Norris can send faxes by stroking his beard close to a phone.

Sega made an arcade game once where you fought Chuck Norris. Every time you put a quarter in, the screen immediately displayed, "You lose." It was Sega's most popular machine ever.

Chuck Norris beat IBM's Deep Blue computer at chess in three moves. He had only a pawn, a thimble, and a checker.

Chuck Norris's penis has its own zip code. At Christmas time it gets more mail than Santa Claus.

The opposite sides of Chuck Norris always add up to seven.

Chuck Norris once lit a fart while camping in the Sahara Forest.

Chuck Norris hit puberty during the second trimester.

Chuck Norris was baptized with napalm.

Chuck Norris's Wikipedia entry has been completely fabricated by the Catholic church.

Chuck Norris has a penis so long that he was the first man to win an Olympic medal for pole vaulting without the use of a pole.

Chuck Norris's nipples can cause severe tire damage.

Chuck Norris can kick a fart back into an ass.

To Chuck Norris, the cup isn't half full or half empty, but always deadly.

Chuck Norris has only one hand: the upper hand.

The only reason Chuck Norris didn't win an Oscar for his performance in *Sidekicks* is because nobody in their right mind would willingly give Chuck Norris a blunt metal object. That's just suicide.

Someone once bet Chuck Norris he couldn't shit on the ceiling. Michelangelo still owes him ten bucks.

Objects in Chuck Norris's rearview mirror appear at their correct distances.

When Chuck Norris had surgery, the anesthesia was applied to the doctors.

Ozzy Osbourne once bit the head off a bat. Not to be outdone, Chuck Norris then bit the head off Batman.

Chuck Norris once brought a man back to life twice and killed him three times because the man had the audacity to die before Chuck Norris was finished killing him.

Chuck Norris's calendar goes straight from March 31st to April 2nd; no one fools Chuck Norris.

Bill Gates lives in constant fear that Chuck Norris's PC will crash.

Chuck Norris visited the Lincoln Memorial and Abe offered him his seat.

If Chuck Norris were a woman, he wouldn't have a period. He would have an exclamation point.

Chuck Norris once struck lightning.

Rosa Parks refused to get out of her seat because she was saving it for Chuck Norris.

As a child, Chuck Norris played Hungry Hungry Hippos with real hippos.

Ghosts are actually caused by Chuck Norris killing people faster than Death can process them.

Chuck Norris never loses a game of Clue, despite the fact everyone knows he's the murderer and used his foot to do it.

Before he goes onstage, Chuck Norris breaks someone's leg to give himself good luck.

Chuck Norris is the only Olympic diver to ever get a gold medal after performing a 1½ somersault with five twists after jumping off his own boner.

The only time Chuck Norris has ever been wrong is the time he thought he had made a mistake.

Chuck Norris once had an erection while lying facedown, and he struck oil.

Chuck Norris cleans the wax out of his ears with a shotgun.

Chuck Norris's driver's license photo looks amazing.

Chuck Norris does not wear a cup. He wears a barrel.

Chuck Norris once ran for Senate in Texas and won
both seats.

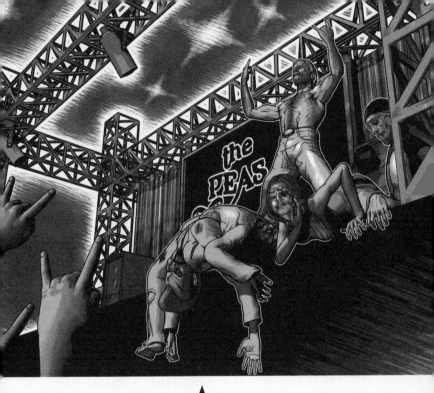

**The Black-Eyed Peas were simply
known as The Peas until they
crossed Chuck Norris.**

When he was a seven-year-old, Chuck Norris's mom once told him to go and dig to China. He left and returned three weeks later with a second-degree black belt in Tae Kwon Do.

When Chuck Norris plays golf, they have to put the hole on the moon.

Chuck Norris is like corn. No matter how much shit he is in he still comes out in one piece.

Chuck Norris built the Panama Canal with one hand.

Chuck Norris was on an episode of *Press Your Luck*. When it was Chuck Norris's turn, he said, "C'mon, no Whammies." No one has since seen another Whammy, nor another episode of *Press Your Luck*.

Mr. T once defeated Chuck Norris in a game of tic-tac-toe. In retaliation, Chuck Norris invented racism.

The one-dollar bill originally had Chuck Norris on it, but the beard kept getting caught in vending machines.

Chuck Norris was born with two umbilical cords, one red and one blue. The bomb squad cut the wrong one.

When Chuck Norris cuts in line, the line bleeds.

Chuck Norris won the Crusades bys T.K.O.

Chuck Norris is a vegetarian—he does not eat animals until he first puts them into vegetative state.

Sometimes, while setting, the sun will linger just a few more minutes on the horizon to get one last look at Chuck Norris.

Chuck Norris ate a box of Alpha-Bits cereal and shat out the entire works of Edgar Allan Poe.

Chuck Norris's mild-mannered alter ego is Superman.

Chuck Norris can kill you in more ways than you know how to die.

Chuck Norris has had his cake and has eaten it, and now he wants yours.

When Chuck Norris eats airplane food, it tastes good.

Chuck Norris once squeezed an M&M so hard that it turned into a Skittle.

Piñatas were made in an attempt to get Chuck Norris to stop kicking the people of Mexico. Sadly this backfired, as all it has resulted in is Chuck Norris now looking for candy after he kicks his victims.

Love means Chuck Norris never has to say he's sorry.

When Superman squeezes a lump of coal, he creates a diamond. When Chuck Norris squeezes a lump of coal, he creates an African child to work in his diamond mines.

One time, Chuck Norris's son went missing. He was found in Chuck Norris's beard two months later.

Chuck Norris once partook in a pissing contest outside of a bar. His opponent drowned.

Chuck Norris is the current reigning World Champion of Yu-Gi-Oh! Cards.

Upon hearing that his good friend, Lance Armstrong, lost his testicles to cancer, Chuck Norris donated one of his to Lance. With just one of Chuck's nuts, Lance was able to win the Tour de France seven times. By the way, Chuck still has two testicles; either he was able to produce a new one simply by flexing, or he had three to begin with. No one knows for sure.

Once, a cobra bit Chuck Norris's leg. After five days of excruciating pain, the cobra died.

Chuck Norris never loses at rock-paper-scissors because he never plays rock-paper-scissors. He plays rock-paper-scissors-roundhouse kick. Chuck Norris never loses at rock-paper-scissors-roundhouse kick.

The Greek pronunciation of Chuck Norris is *Zeus*.

Somewhere, right now, Chuck Norris is plowing a woman he doesn't love.

Chuck Norris went to college on an affirmative-action scholarship. Nobody objected.

Upon arriving on the moon, Neil Armstrong caught a 382,500-kilometer touchdown pass from Chuck Norris. ⟶

Chuck Norris's real name is Switchblade Killingsworth. He changed it to Chuck Norris because it sounded tougher.

Give MacGyver a toothpick and a pocketknife and he'll escape from handcuffs. Give Chuck Norris the same tools and he'll win a war, climb Mount Everest, and build a new mansion while carrying around a pocketknife and a toothpick.

Chuck Norris once thought he was stuck between a rock and a hard place. He quickly realized he was standing between two mirrors.

Chuck Norris once put on a pair of roller skates and showed up at a quarry looking for a job. He is now the most powerful dump truck known to man.

Chuck Norris is the only person on the planet who can kick you in the back of the face.

Chuck Norris is always on top during sex because Chuck Norris never fucks up.

Never use the phrase "eat my heart out" around Chuck Norris. He will.

Chuck Norris once broke a mirror on a black cat under a ladder on Friday the 13th. He won the lottery later that day.

On the comments part in Chuck Norris's first-grade report card, it said, "What Mr. Norris lacks in social skills he makes up for in the bedroom."

Chuck Norris deeply admires and respects the mountain goat.

The jihadists are pissed because they can no longer tell their recruits to expect seventy-three virgins in heaven. The best they can now do is seventy-three women who have already had sex with Chuck Norris. ⟶

Chuck Norris slept through 9/11. His bedroom was on the 73rd floor.

The only match for Chuck Norris is the one he burns you with.

Chuck Norris builds all the Home
Depots with his bare hands.

The term *heartburn* was invented when Chuck Norris
roundhouse kicked a man in the chest and his heart caught
fire.

Men once believed that Chuck Norris revolved around the earth; today we know the opposite to be true, and the terrible price those fools paid for their ignorance.

Pictures of Chuck Norris are worth two thousand words.

When Chuck Norris looks in a mirror, the mirror shatters, because not even glass is stupid enough to get in between Chuck Norris and Chuck Norris.

Death once had a near–Chuck Norris experience.

Chuck Norris doesn't sleep.
He waits.

Acknowledgments

Very special thanks, of course, to my family. Without their continued support, you wouldn't be reading any of this.

To my friends: I'm contractually allowed only ten free copies of this book and you're not getting any of them.

Big thank-yous to Charlotte Wasserstein from WMA for getting me hooked on this book project again and walking me through the publishing process, as well as to my editor, Patrick Mulligan from Gotham, for being so enthusiastic about the project and being able to see eye to eye with me on everything.

And **of course to Chuck:** You've got an awesome sense of humor. Thanks for playing along.

About the Author

Ian Spector is an undergraduate at Brown University, where he studies neuroscience and edits the campus humor magazine. He created the original Chuck Norris Fact Generator Web site, starting the Chuck Norris Fact phenomenon. A survivor of a real-life encounter with Chuck Norris himself, Spector divides his time between school in Providence, Rhode Island, and home on Long Island.